C000084928

Further up the River

and fifty other poems

Kevin Pyne

"Kevin Pyne's poems are powerful and original, his images unexpected and perceptive. He evokes with equal tenderness his love for his dead wife and his love of the river and the sea. I believe anyone who reads them will be both touched and profoundly moved by his passion."
David Dimbleby

"I recommend these poems above all to anyone who wants to do more than blow through a place, anyone who has time to sit down and listen a little more deeply to one of the west's true voices."
Alice Oswald, Winner of the 2002 T.S. Eliot Prize

"This is a book of tough unsentimental poems
...an astonishing success in countryside publishing."
Bill Taylor, Editor, Countryman

"A beautiful celebration of Westcountry life...
a tonic for anyone with preconceptions about the world of poetry, the book is quite simply devoid of pretension."
Vicky Sartain, Devon Today

"A perfect read...the poems are powerful and original and are written with a deep understanding of his work, love and the Westcountry."
Devon Life

"I didn't make it to the end of the first poem. I had to put the book down because the tears were blinding me...this (is a) compassionate work of art..."
Bob Curtis, Herald Express

"A must for your bookshelf."
Hilary Bastone, Herald Express

"Undoubted ability to put his words into powerful and perceptive poetry..."
Colin Bradley, Western Morning News

"I have read and re-read the poems. I imagine I will be doing so for many years to come. They are a source of great enjoyment."
Jude Chilvers, Sunday Independent

"I haven't lost the love of my life, I don't have a long and passionate history with the coves and waterways of Dartmouth, I don't row and I don't have children...that was until I read Kevin Pyne's poetry and then I'm right there with him, feeling everything he feels, seeing it all through his eyes."
Judi Spiers, BBC Radio Devon

Further up the River

and fifty other poems

Kevin Pyne

Richard
Webb

AUTHOR'S DEDICATION

You loved me for the unexpected

Published in the United Kingdom in 2004 by Richard Webb
First impression October 2004
Second impression November 2004
Third impression June 2005
Fourth impression May 2007

Copyright © Kevin Pyne 2004

Foreword © Alice Oswald 2004

The right of Kevin Pyne to be identified as the author of this work has been
asserted by him in accordance with the Copyright, Designs and Patents Act, 1988

This book is sold subject to the condition that it shall not, by way of trade or
otherwise circulated without the publisher's prior consent in any form of binding
or cover other than that in which it is published and without a similar condition
including this condition being imposed on the subsequent purchaser

Designed by Laurence Daeche, Anon Design Co., Christchurch, Dorset

A CIP catalogue record for this book is available from the British Library

ISBN 978-0953636129

Typeset in 14/14pt Perpetua

Printed and bound in the United Kingdom by Short Run Press, Exeter, Devon

RW.UK Ltd trading as Richard Webb, Publisher

Richard Webb, Publisher
Dartmouth, Devon, England

KEVIN PYNE

Kevin Pyne was born in Dartmouth, Devon in 1950. His father was from an old Dartmouth family, his mother from County Sligo, Ireland and he has two sisters. Educated at St. Cuthbert Mayne, Torquay, Kevin left school at 16 and has since worked as a boatman and ferryman on the river Dart for over 35 years.

Having to leave the ferry due to an accident at work, Kevin turned his attention to helping found the Dart Gig Club and is now an umpire on the Cornish pilot gig circuit.

He has combined this with a love of photography and has a reputation for his fine rowing pictures which, in addition to the Westcountry, he has taken in the USA, France, Holland and the Isles of Scilly.

Kevin's life has always been on or near the water and he has a special attachment to all the ports and harbours of the Westcountry and respects all those who make their living from the sea.

After nearly 30 years of marriage Kevin was widowed in 1999 when his brave and beautiful wife Lyzie died of cancer, aged only 46. Their two children are both Maritime Business graduates of the University of Plymouth – Ross is now a chartered shipbroker and Robyn is studying for her Ph.D.

Misfortune struck Kevin again in 2002 when he nearly died from the life-threatening flesh-eating disease, necrotising fasciitis, which has left him partly disabled.

After his six months in hospital he became a founder member of the Devon flag group and this green flag with a white cross can now be seen flying proudly all over Devon, like its black and white counterpart in Cornwall, both counties being part of the ancient Celtic kingdom of Dumnonia.

Kevin's experiences of observing the ever-changing life on the river, his love of the people and history of the Westcountry, the tragic loss of his wife and his own brush with death, have all shaped and coloured the many varied poems that appear in his first published work *Further up the River*.

Ken Pyne

FOREWORD

I was lucky to meet Kevin Pyne back in 1999, when he took me down to Old Mill Creek in his boat, with his dog. I remember him quoting long chunks of Kipling and Causley as he handled the tiller - there was no mistaking his passionate connection to poetry.

The impression I formed of him then, as someone not only genuinely awake to poetry, but also full to the brim and overflowing with things to say about the river, the sea beyond and his late wife Lyzie comes back to me now when I read his poems. I love their abundance, their unpompousness and their routed knowledge of one place. I love the way they sound just like kept back pieces of his conversation, though with a sure sense of rhythm and shape.

Like so many places, the south-west is filling up with holiday homes and its boatyards are turning into marinas for rich men's yachts. Kevin has seen the places as they were half a century ago, with big working ships and a close community and he is very much a part of its proud tradition of boat-handling, sea-watching and fiery types. Those of us who come artfully or artily to his river can learn a lot from him. What detail there is in a poem like *China clay*.

My favourites are *Joyce Gundry's fruitcake, China clay,* and *Sky field* but I recommend these poems above all to anyone who wants to do more than blow through a place, anyone who has time to sit down and listen a little more deeply to one of the west's true voices.

Alice Oswald

PREFACE

A while ago I asked, a journalist, if she believed as I do, in mermaids. Her answer will stay with me always: she said 'I believe in magic'.

How can an ex-ferryman, who can't spell, be naïve enough to think he is a poet? The answer is love. The love of a beautiful woman I lost by way of her untimely death from cancer. I feel that the parting gift from my late wife is my ability to put my words into poetry. The hurt that I felt on Lyzie's death has manifested itself into a greater sense of understanding, which is reflected in my poetry. I never felt anger for her loss. I am grateful for the love and time that we shared together.

All through the time Lyzie lay ill in the cottage hospital here in Dartmouth, two young dolphins played day after day in the river just outside the hospital. On the night she died those same two dolphins swam away. They were never seen again. Yes, I believe in magic. I believe they took her for a mermaid. An hour after her death I walked along the banks of the Dart and I realized that in the blue and silver moonlight of the early hours of the morning, nothing in the grief or happiness a mortal man can feel, will affect the awesome and uncontrollable surge of the river as it runs to the sea. Life goes on; I would go on. I resolved that I would give thanks for all that she had gifted me and not become bitter and resentful.

Lyzie gave us two beautiful children, who at times needed me to be both their mum and dad. Yet when I almost died a while ago, they became mum and dad to me. I wrote the poem *Further up the River* to explain to them where I thought their mum had gone. Ever since then poems seem to pour from me.

My love of the Westcountry and its people are reflected in my poetry. I have a fascination and a passion for rowing. I love ships, boats, heavy machinery and indeed all boy-like things.

I feel that my life-long interest in photography has done much to sharpen my eye. I am able to see beauty in the simplest things and I hope translate that beauty into verse.

I grew up around the harbourside and banks of the river Dart. My children were brought up in the same way. I am very lucky; rarely have I done anything that I did not wish to do. As a family we picnicked and played in the shadow of the Royal Naval College here in Dartmouth – in Old Mill Creek, where princes and princesses played no greater or lesser games. We swam, we rowed, we laughed and we loved each other.

Although Dartmouth and the river Dart are special to me, the harbours and villages in the south-west are also my dreaming grounds. They all have the same comfortable feel to me. It makes little difference which sea port you are in; a man in dirty yellow waterproof leggings is the same man whether he lives in Penzance or Weymouth – his hopes are also the same as my hopes and fears. The same strong pretty girls row out on a summer's evening

I see my lack of a formal education as a huge advantage - because I do not know what the rules are I am not constrained by what I see as my potential poetical subject matter.

My Catholic upbringing makes me inclined to tell the truth and this perhaps sometimes puts me at a disadvantage. I write about ordinary people in ordinary situations. My descriptions are always frank

I resent the demise of a way of life which, although simple, separates the Westcountry men and women from those of the rest of the country. It does not make us in any way better than our fellow countrymen. However, I feel we retain an empathy with such things as the water, the sea and the land.

To me, the Westcountry has the feel of a painting. Some people look in upon it while others are the characters featured in and beyond the canvas. I feel this imagery particularly applies to the people of the water.

As children, we were cast loose like moorland cattle every summer and not rounded up again until September for school. I come from the last generation to always have had grazed knees and to be covered in scratches and nettle stings. I always seemed to have wet feet and to smell of fish. I have never lost that childlike perception. I listened to old people tell stories of the old ways and learnt from people who had the time to teach.

Please share with me my poems, my thoughts and dreams. I hope that you too will find peace, solace and fun in them, as I have. I take great pleasure from the simple things around me.

Come with me, if you will, we won't ever be that far away and it's all right to drift and dream. Leave for a few moments, the madness which seems to be the world at times today. Just pinch an hour and let's go, perhaps for just a while, a little further up the river!

Kevin Pyne

CONTENTS

love

water

love

Further up the River

It's no use you looking, I am gone
We have said our last goodbyes,
It was my time, we did not fail.
I will watch you, can only watch you from afar;
Free from pain
As certain as our river runs to the sea,
I will be there
Each ship that you see, I will see
Each oar's sweep, and stroke, I will hear
Search all that you will, I cannot return to you
Chase me, call me, I cannot come to you
I am you see, further up the river
Though I cherish your memory
Will forever feel your last kiss
No matter how hard you row, mile after heart aching mile,
I will be just in front of you, a memory
Only when you bow your tired head,
Weary of the chase, perhaps decades duly passed,
Then and only then, can I rest besides you
Further up the river, when you row with fever spent,
Stop, slump, lose all momentum.
Quickly, I will steady you, comfort you, take your side again,
This time for ever

On the death of Lyzie 23rd September 1999.

At the cove

And seeing you were alone
The only sound the hiss of pebbles
Caught in the rush and turn of the wave
You stripped
Walked through the dappled sunlight out into the sea
As your fingers touched the still rising tide
The swell gently rose to greet you
Lifting and surrounding you
Until with a gasp you were swimming
I jointed you later, dropping anchor
You swam out to meet me
Through the blue green summer sea
I saw that you were naked
Nervously I told you that you would be caught
What would they think
You simply laughed
Teased me for being a prude
Swam around
Delighting in my discomfort
Laughing, goading me
Wet hair, redder even than the cliffs
Your pale skin the colour of a church candle
Beneath the shimmering water
The sea like cellophane
Sealing your image beneath it
Embarrassed by my thoughts

I dived in and gasped
Not wanting to condone your behaviour
Swimming into the shore
You were not so long behind me
I walked to meet you
Towel in hand, I watched you naked
So small, so perfect, so firm
Until your smiling blue eyes told me I was staring
As I wrapped your shivering body in a towel
You stood so still like a child at bath time stands
Almost trance like, eyes as blue as blue
I rubbed you dry
You let me rub you dry
I was pretending to be cross
Shaking my head in disbelief
Loving every second

Isn't it every man's dream?

Near death

I almost came to meet you
I saw you in my dreams
Standing where the warm green waters
Touch the bowing oaks at autumn time
At first I didn't see you there
Your so so long red hair
Still hides you in the autumn foliage
Until you smiled, shook your head
And said without any hint of sadness
"No not yet"
I remembered then your nervous laugh
As in your soft gentle voice
You whispered to me that I should
"Go on back"
Be among the ones that we still love
So I smiled, turned and left you
Where the seals go
And dolphins swim

Just a little further up the river

After I nearly died.

Dressing gown

When you died I parcelled up your things
And gave them all away
I hated throwing out your underwear
I felt sad for the memories
Glad for your lack of pain
But above all I missed you
Early one morning I heard a noise
I could not send you to look
So I had to go
Hanging outside the wardrobe was your big blue dressing gown
So I put it on and crept downstairs
There was nothing there
There never is!
It was daft I know but it felt so comfortable
And it was for either sex
So now I wear it all the time
It snuggles all around me just like you did
And I think of you naked having just slipped out of bed
I wonder just where your breasts would be
I loved your breasts almost as much
As I loved your autumn beech red hair
And a glimpse of your leg when you went to make the tea always
Got me excited
I feel better when I put it on
I hope you don't mind

I wonder how many other people have done the same thing?

Empty bras

Empty bras
Don't mean a lot
A drawer full of empty bras
Is all I've got
They are all so small
Like dead balloons
Lie there still on afternoons
Once you filled them
Just so right
Dark as dark
White as white
Empty bras in an empty drawer
Left they're to haunt me evermore…

It took me four years to empty her underwear drawer.

Fiddler in the graveyard

Never to dance is to die
There are no sad tunes
No laments
Only reels and jigs
In my memories of you
The fiddler comes
Instead of cut flowers
To play at your graveside
I never think of you without smiling
I miss watching you dancing
You loved me for the unexpected
So a fiddler plays at your graveside

I asked a busker who was playing the violin if she would mind popping into the cemetery on her way home to play a tune for Lyzie and occasionally I ask musicians to go up to her grave and play a tune or two.

It was almost a dance

Naked
Almost a dance
No beyond dance
Always the same I watched fascinated
Loved to watch
I could do no other
First brush always from your forehead
Lifting, tilting your head
Right back
Until your still wet hair
Hung down below your shoulder blades
As you stared fixated almost trance-like into the mirror
I would wonder
Where do women's thoughts go when they brush their hair
Across the left side
Head pulling down and left
Then across the right side
Head pulling down and right
Each time the moments almost violent
The repetitive drone of the hair dryer the only accompaniment
As you shifted in to banks and turns of muscular combinations
Which I found mesmerising, erotic
When it was done
The encore

Throwing your head forward
With such a force before
Brushing your hair from underneath forwards
As if a minor bird in courtship
Covering your breasts
The little strawberry mark exposed
In the nape of your neck
A girl's figure so perfect
A woman's composure
And there for me to see
Your beautiful hair as red as any sunset
Copper beech hair so thick
That I could not breathe
If you chose to make love to me
But then quickly as if anticipating my thoughts
You were dressed and were gone
Popping like a firework
Into the day ahead

Watching Lyzie dry her hair.

Lady in green

My love is a lady in green
She has hair the colour of our red fields
She rises to meet me with the sun
And leaves me with the long shadow
In the last light of summer to sleep
A winter's sleep
My love is a lady in green
Who lays all before me in silence
Her red hair the colour of a Devon valley beach
To which the dews of autumn give lustre
Yet dark auburn when the soft rains come
The red of fire when the March winds blow
And softly dry her locks
My love is a lady in green
When in spring she becomes again the very tilth of life
My love is a lady in green
Who has eyes for no one
Save the azure of the blue sea
Folding itself in upon her shores
My love is a lady in green
She who gives me the great gift
Of her jewels shimmering in the sunlight
Her sands her sea her woodlands
Her moorland brow
Standing cold and stark
Naked as she stands unmoved by wind and storm

Since the earth's first cooling crust
Wrapped her in its blanket at her beginning
My love is a lady in green so beautiful
Each given mile a gemstone of joy
That I may love her always is with out question
I stand silent enraptured by her beauty
And I find new pleasure at her being
In every given day
My love is a lady in green
I lay safe within her harbours
Until the storms are gone, until they are spent
Until it is safe, and I can set forth again
Across her warm pulsing seas
My love is a lady in green
She gives up her bounty
That I may prosper
My love is a lady in green
She who is as old as time
And yet as young as tomorrow ...

A poem to Devon the county I love and in which I was born.

My young maid's a Devon maid

My young maid's a Devon maid
Pale skinned like Teign valley clay
She's soft and kind like our countryside
I wouldn't have her any other way

I met her walking on Dartmoor
Upon Saint Petroc's day
She was climbing up and over Haytor rock
When I was going the other way

She likes to swim in the waters blue
At first light on a summers morn
If I did not know it different
I would swear a merry maid I had born.

My young maid's a Devon maid
She has eyes the colour of our sea
And earrings the shape of Devon flags
That I did give to she

She has hair the colour of August wheat
It shimmers in the warm sunshine
And a smile that beams like the Start Point light
When seen from Slapton line

She set up house in Plymouth town
She loves to sing and row
She waves goodbye as the ships sail out
From way up on Plymouth Hoe

And I will give her Devon cream
With scones and strawberry jam
And a glass of cider clear
When we row up for cockles and plums at Dittisham

My girl's a Devon Maid
She has sailed the mighty sea
She was born and bred in Dartmouth town
And has a nautical degree.

*A parody on Charles Causley's **My Young Man's a Cornishman** -
a poem I love and which my daughter Robyn read to me again and again
when I almost died in Derriford hospital (Robyn was in the final year
of her maritime degree course).*

Blue line

I sent a message that I miss you
Down the thin blue line
You sent me back a message
Saying you were doing fine
Doing fine without me
And getting all that you could get
It only took three seconds
How I hate the internet!

Written after an argument with a good friend.

Plum light

Skins likened to velvet
Dusty purple
Rich deep dark purple
That in the mid August
And when the nine o'clock
Would see lovers lost
To the dark
In the orchard
The plum is ripe
And in the plum light
Of the August moon
Where summer lovers lay so still
The tree would hold a lover's gift
Picked so soft
So tender beneath its branches

A certain plum tree in a secret corner on the river Dart.

A round turn and two half hitches

A round turn and two half hitches
Ties my life to you
Yes, there have been many glitches
But the rope stayed strong and true
Even when the storms came
The rope stayed long and strong
But I had to let the rope go
When you closed your eyes to leave
It's a strong rope and a long rope
Which took our lives to reeve
So I'll splice your end to my end
Even if the rope is half as long
I will never splice another
But the rope is twice as strong...

I was sat in my boat store one day and the poem came to me. The initial draft was written on a scrap piece of wood.

Port side aft

I will come again to you
Sit with you
Watch you work
Because I liked to watch you
But this time you won't have to tell me to
"Keep out of the way"
As you always did in another time
Even though
I knew you only told me because you loved me
I liked being told
Port side aft
Leave me a little room
I will be there
As you work in your baggy yellow leggings
You will know
I will watch in silence
Put my hand on your hand as you steer
For even though we can not be together
Touch
Our meetings
Held in silence will be understood
Leave just a little room for me please
As you always did
Port side aft...

A poem for dreamers.

She was the better person

I lost her when the leaves fell
She withered, closed her eyes and blew away
I knew that I would one day lose her
Understood she could not stay
She had no life to hold her
And I knew I could not reach
When her breath it left her
I said goodbye and kissed her
I touched her hair of copper winter beech
I left her in the midnight
When the breeze blew dry and cold
Walked out to see the river
Its secrets run so deep and untold
Those silver lines of sorrow
Mixed with the ebbing sea
I thanked the gleaming rising moonlight
For what she had meant to me
And I watch the mighty river
As the dolphins swam away
Knowing they had taken her
For a mermaid on that day
On the day she died and left me
I felt her metamorphose
Where the river meets the sea
I gave her back to my god, her father
The great and mighty sea

For the sea so calm and gentle
It had once offered me a trade
I traded love for sorrow
And time with a pretty mermaid
So when I row the river
As the waves gently hiss and roll
I still feel her close besides me
And have warmth within my soul...

Walking the banks of the Dart on the night she died.

The wooden horse

In an airless lightless corridor
The wooden horse rocks
To keep the noisy children's dreams
In childhood
We sit strangers
Reading dog-eared magazines
Remembering nothing of what we read
Remembering only the lines of blue chairs
Against the bare washed walls
That seem to go on forever
But there is no forever
Only the wooden horse is forever
Its tail pulled thin
Its mane pulled thin
The grey dappled paint can be replaced
Riders will come and go
Sticky shoed nurses will pass by
In silence
Squeaking their way along the polished corridors
Day after day
Patients are told their fate
A smile for some
For others tears

You left thoughtfully in dignified silence
Past the wooden horse without a name
Who never leaves, and cannot die
Strangely though I wish it life
Even though life is for a term...

The little wooden rocking horse in the corridor outside the surgery consultation rooms at Torbay hospital on the day Lyzie was told her cancer was terminal.

Rowing the white boat

Spring takes longer to come
Each year
Sometimes like today
The winter puts on its jewellery
Today the skies were blanket blue
It a special day
A day for the white boat
I talk lots never meaning what I say
That is unless I am rowing
Then I row in silence
To special places
And even if I can't say it
Please understand what I can't say
No one rows the white boat
Unless I care for them…

My little white dinghy is one of the most precious things I have.

I left my heart in the Co-op

I left my heart in the Co-op
It's down by the margarine
I didn't mean to leave it
It just got sort of stuck in between
I saw her there
By the freezer
She looked a lot like you
Only she was thirty years younger
And I was fifty-two
I didn't mean to stare though
As she smiled
Then turned away
But the marge and my heart were made
From sunflowers
I got two for one that day...

*I was shopping and a beautiful little red-head probably thirty years my
younger gave me a huge smile.*

The washing line

I never use the washing line
Even when the sun it shines
I know just why
It's 'cos your not there
To grace the yard with your underwear
Which seemed to fly
Like signal flags
How I miss that beautiful lingerie on a sunny day
And I would rather keep the dream that way
Why then would I have cared about
Our neighbours sniggers
When I was reading I love you
In sexy bras and knickers...

18th June 2003 my birthday would have been our
32nd wedding anniversary.

Bluebell wood

Sing a song for springtime
Lance it through my heart
Just a song for springtime
Let us never be apart
Let us love as lovers
For ever if we can
And you be a gentle woman
I a gentle man
Sing a song a May song
When the bluebells are in flower
And let us walk as lovers walk
Hour after hour
Hour after hour through the blue haze
As the spring leaves
Turn a lighter shade of green
If I cannot tell you, I love you
Though I love you is
Exactly what I mean

*Written as Dart Music Festival was in progress and I just thought
I should try to write a song.*

⚓ ⚓ ⚓ *water* ⚓ ⚓ ⚓

River dogs

We work the river all the time
My old dog and me
We don't much mix with others
They only hurt you see
So we keep ourselves to ourselves
And do just what we can
And the both of us we understand
What makes an honest man
She's not a young dog now you see
And others treated her cruel
She'd bite you if you came too close
But then I know the rule
She'd rather be with my late wife
How we loved her gentle voice
And I always know now she's gone
That I am second choice
But all I've got is my old dog
And all she's got is me
That the way it is for us
And that's the way it'll be...

To my dog, Ceilidh.

Blue boats

Blue boats like
Blue birds tossing in among the storm
Come home again the blue boats
To the fires warm
Yellow figures bright as lights
Held in among the spume
Bring them home again tonight
Those blue boats
Bring my love
Safe into this room…

There is a family of fishermen comprising three brothers.
This poem is dedicated to them.

Christmas harbour

The ferry's on the moorings
The ferryman's asleep
He waited up for Santa Claus
To cross the waters deep

Bells across the water
On the Christmas tide
Hear the bells ringing across the river wide
Sunlight on the water upon this golden Christmas morn
Tells the seals and dolphins of a baby who is born
No need to tell the mermaids
Whilst they comb their pretty hair
They listen to the children
There is laughter everywhere

And if out beyond the harbour
There should be a mighty storm
Pray for those brave mariners
And keep them safe and warm
Let the bells guide them into harbour
Wherever that may be
Or let them sail on Christmas day
Across a clear blue sea...

For all those who have to work over Christmas.

Clean sweep

They were miners in their hard hats
Cornish men in the main
Tough men in overalls
Who buried in the pipes and drains
Mining engineers for the mostly
Schooled in Camborne town
Who bury the nation's unwanted
Way way below the ground
Beneath the streets and hillsides
They worked the miner's way
I would meet them at the snack hut
Having a break for tea
They told me they cleaned up Cornwall
They would do the same for me
As on they drilled with great precision
Underneath the earth and sea
Until they crossed our river
With a pipe which was never seen
Then filled in the hole
And left it there
As if they had never been
They talked in millimetres
Never seeming to get it wrong
Four centimetres was all they were out
Through bedrock
On a pipe almost a mile long

"How's it going?" I asked them
As we drank our mugs of tea
"Finished this week by Thursday"
Came the proud reply to me
Then they jumped back in the crew cab
Shouted a warm goodbye
Then left me a cleaner river
In days as blue as the sky
I think of them as the sunsets
As the dolphins and seals return to call
Those lads who cleaned up the south-west
In their dirty overalls.

Written by way of thanks to the gangs who laid miles of pipe for South West Water's 'Clean Sweep' programme of waste water treatment throughout Devon and Cornwall.

Elizabeth Mary

She filled her foresail
Until it bloomed out like a pregnant woman's life-filled belly
Cradling the wind deep into her canvas womb
Her boom ran out until it skimmed across the water's edge
Drowning the trailing sheets on every wave
This was sailing that I could understand
A foot up on the combing
Until we heaved the wind into her
Gathered it up into her sails
And set alight her wooden soul
Sing water, water sing
As she cuts threw the cat's-paws
Releasing our joyous souls
From the penance of her keep
Drive on *Elizabeth Mary*
Tease the angry scolding wind before it dies
As we race toward the lifting sun
Leave our happy laughter in your boiling wake
Race on until you cross the sea of time
Where blocks not stainless winches
Arrest the elements
Cup them in your salt-etched sails
Drive on *Elizabeth Mary*
Our sou'westers and oilskins
Drenched in the sea spume

Our cold hands paying out and pulling in
Letting us share with the ghosts in your past
Feeling you drive on through our finger tips
Hold in the wind *Elizabeth Mary*
And steal another knot
From the wind's purse
As you dance the gaffer's dance
On this a new clear spring morning...

The best day's sailing I've ever had in my life.

Gigs on the beach

I don't want to stand in Leicester Square
When the crowds rush by my heart's not there
London for me is out of reach
I'd rather watch gleaming coloured
Pilot gigs all lined up on the beach

Willi Peters, Lantic, Corsair, Mystery
These are the names that mean to me
That I'm back home in my beloved Westcountry,
Midst silver sands and azure blue seas

No London life is not for me
You can keep your posh shows and new Mercedes-Benz
I belong where no one dresses up or pretends
For the only show I need to see
Is the bright red sun dipping beneath a golden sea

I'll stay down west with my rowing friends
All the money in the world can't make amends
A credit card or a large bank note
Can't make you feel as one with the boat
Can't make you feel part of the sea

Not for me the posh bistro
When they sing down Cadgwith soft and low
I'll be way down west for an evening row
From St Mary's pool past Crow Bar to Tresco
'Cos I'm never happier than when I row

Past *Bonnet*, and *Tregarthens* out in the Sound
Hear the lasses laughing rowing lightly, homeward bound
To the clicking pin and the creaking leather
Keeping an eye for the wind, an eye for the weather

Up past Loe beach and Birdy's Devoran shed
Falmouth to Trura is just a way ahead
It's a choppy little swell, an' it's been an' 'ard old day
The *Morlader* or the *Royal* will take me forth
Or the *Dasher* and *Teaser* if I'm up north

Mother, father, brother, daughter
Row out from Rame past the Plymouth breakwater
And if I am in the bay off St Ives
The *Porthminster* sails home with Kernow's wives

And if I cross to Devon where the flags are green
There's the gigs on the Tamer in between
Catalina and *Mary Newman* the flying machine!
They're all kind of colours in Weymouth town
And they drink so much beer that a man might drown

They'll row any darn thing at all, up Dartmouth way
Lightning and *Volante* are first away
As they race down the river for Lyzie rouge la fée
Past Britannia boys and girls coming the other way
In the valley by the sea which runs away from the moors

They'd rather have a row on the Yealm
Than have stayed indoors
Even if the age of the crew tots up to four hundred and four
And the *Wolf*, it stalks the Salcombe shores

You can keep your cities and your taxi cabs
These things mean nothing to me
I'm not all up for grabs
Fly, Morvoren, Isis, Speculation, Rose, St Elvin, Lark,
I don't need to take a stroll in Regents Park

I could not wish or ask for more
When the air is still on a calm lee shore
Than to be out at sea pulling away
Thinking of a pint and a song at the end of the day
As I drag my favourite oar through, - again and again
As the coxswain screams "give me ten hard ones" it's only pain

Until it's easy up and we're back on land
And I hear her keel, take the soft white sand
And I jump out quick to steady her, and offer a hand
To a smiling girl or a mate I knew from school
Knowing my strong arm and oar
Are my only tools…

I follow pilot gig rowing with a passion - it has made me many friends!
Local dialect has been used for some of the place names.

Regatta rowing

Oh my arms are hurting
And my back is fit to break
Why do I ever want to row at regatta?
Tell me for pity sake
My head it hurts from all that drinking
And lord knows I need to my earn my keep
But I was out till half past one
Then could I get to sleep
My mind was on the river
And my heart began to race
I've just got to be first over the line
Who remembers second place
I've a million things to do this morning
I've to shop and cook and wash
Then it's off down to the bank again
To load up with more dosh
But don't you see I love it
It's the same thing every year
She's a better rower than she is
He should hang up his oar
Oh please don't shake my hand too hard
And oh my bum is sore
Have you remembered to sign in?
He's not good enough for that crew
So and so hasn't turned up
And now what do we do

We're not taking him on he couldn't pull a bun out of a bag
Well go and run and find them
Can someone give us a fag!
All the wind-ups and arguments
Who could miss them for the entire world
Yet in that ten minutes of agony and anguish
If perform as well as I might
The pain and misery and the agony
Of a hard day's rowing slip away quickly and fade out of sight
Mother daughter sister brother
Aunty uncle wife
The pride that I feel and the friends that I make
On rowing days at regatta
Stay with me for the rest of my life

To all rowers everywhere.

Light airs

They left at eight, well at quarter past
To wash the city out of themselves
Outward on the ebb
On a crisp honey coloured September tide
A teaser's day that the west keeps for its own
Too far for the tourists to come
Only one day of brightness
Between bookends of grey and wet
The river was as empty as Christmas day
Our red sails like the red cows
Were set, then made no hurry in the light wind
We sailed our thoughts out of us
We sailed our laughter in
We sailed our warmth and friendships back into us
Light airs light talk "watch out for the ferries"
Past the castles and the grey green
Of St Petrox where the headstones
Keep a watch over the river mouth
Until we reached the long line
Of the beach at Slapton
As the wind just dropped away
As our minds cleared away
We hunted the locker for the hand lines
Stole a supper of silver harvest mackerel
Ate our lunch had a pee and drifted
Elbows over the combing leaning lazy backed

Looking up into empty sail hour on hour
Our blood not flowing for a while with the madness
Of the money world
Instead with the rhythms warm late summer sea
We faced the Start white lighthouse
Watched the sheep like snowflakes
In among the copper coloured ferns and short grass
Looked all along the great rocks
Fell silent like the ghosts of the villagers at Hallsands
There was no tax to pay on this day
Nothing would be taken from our life's allotted days
Suddenly the wind appeared from its rest
She came alive healed us awake
Flicking the plastic cups into the cockpit
Mewstone open of the high land on Down End Point
Then ease her in past the Home Stone buoy
Clip the Black Stone and pick up the flood for home
Until the wind bids us a good evening
Leaves us to drift up past the belly of the river
And wave from the ferryman
Past the great flagstaffed red-bricked Naval College
Whose clock sounds out in ship's bells,
Whose clock hands are too small to see
Until the green oaks pick up their long shadows
In the evening light beyond the picket boats at Sandquay
Beyond the dead shipyard with its rust brown corpses

Until the bells in distant villages
Tingle in our minds and hang in the air like the wood smoke
From someone's river banked baked cooked supper
Light airs for light days
In which sea tired happy people are content
In the knowledge
That they have pinched a day from life's tally
And kept it for themselves

Written for a person who simply loves to sail.

Sky field

The grass will be long
In the sky field
Where ships pass in the distance
As boats pass below
The sky field will be empty
As empty as the town below
In the morning in the sky field
The brown hare awaits
The rooks watch
The buzzards call
But no one comes to the sky field
And best thoughts
I have none
They grow only in the sky field
Where people below
Cannot sense them
As ships pass
As my thoughts pass
To the sky field in the morning...

Not being able to walk in the fields above my home with
Sarah Flint during the Foot and Mouth epidemic.

The ferryman

All set to seaward
Save one I know
Who back and forward
Must he go
Until he comes to end his day
When he goes back the other way
To sit in silence by the sea
The sea that has no time for he
And think on what he's done this day
And who he fetched to earn his pay
The crying widow
The baby born
The gleaming hearse
On the breaking dawn
The lovers lost
The giggling school girls
The spotty boys
Anxious to try out other toys
All are born for what it costs
The happy drunkard a fisherman
When will they ever learn
Not to give away the cash they earn
To cross the river there perhaps and back
The rushing blushing housewife who stayed to long
Embraced in someone else's arms

The curate in her robes of black
The merchant seaman and the happy jack
Set to cross again the angry sea
For all will cross the Lower Ferry
For the wind doth blow
And the ship doth roll
But it will not bother he
For he's the corporation ferryman
And he will never go to sea…

Twenty five years of my life – they only give you fifteen for murder!

There's a ship in the river

There's a ship in the river
There are strangers upon her deck
They lean and stare
We lean and stare
We wonder
They wonder
Pilot boats come and go
Ship's boats come and go
Old men say those were the days
Young men say these are the days
Everything's best china
When there's a ship in the river...

Dartmouth never seems right unless there's a ship in the river and the town is functioning as a proper harbour should.

St. Petrox church

Who first layered stone on stone
To form a shelter
Where the dark Dart's moorlands waters first reach the sea
Who then set the light in tower high
To guide them in
The seaman to the calm
That they may pray and give thanks
To that good saint who gave his name
To each holy place where he had rested
And when the storm winds rage
Let them sing and be safe
Closed in above the mighty sea
Until again it is time
To make a passage forth
To seaward of the grey stone church
Where all those who must sail away
Have for centuries
Waved with a hesitant hand
A last goodbye to their
Loved ones gathered to pray
For their safe return
Pray that they may hear the bell for evensong
Ring out across the water once again...

A poem on 4th June, St Petroc's day – a favourite walk, a favourite church.
The spelling of the church in Dartmouth is St. Petrox but elsewhere St. Petrock or St. Petroc.
He is a Celtic Saint with many churches dedicated to him throughout Devon and Cornwall.

Tipper's Quay

The saints and souls of sinners
Get blasted out to sea
By a rusting brown old cannon
Which in Sebastopol should be
The sun it fires up slowly
As though the cannon had shot it forth
And prises back the morning
From the freezing cold dry north

The ferry's come alongside
Beyond the harbour wall
They'll be setting off soon to cross the river
It takes no time at all
The flags fly stiff as cardboard
The green and white and black
As the ferry tug crosses over
Soon it will be back
The radio in the ferry wheelhouse
Gives a jingled out report
It's a mixture of radio pop jingles
And Brixham trawler talk

The gleaming black old hearse
Shines in the still rising warming sun
The ferry will bring a new born baby back into town
Before the day gets done
Nothing changes quickly
In the town beside the sea
As the ghosts who laid out the toe-rag
Walk the Tipper's Quay

Orion rises over his Warfleet
As the squawking kittiwakes rise high
To fish under the neon lamp
In the blue dark starlit bird-filled sky
The souls of thoughtful pilgrims
Wander past the old Marine
Where the drinkers who are turned to dust
No longer find a song to sing
They were boarding for America
Five centuries ago at noon
As a slow old stealthy heron
Jumps up and flies across the climbing moon ...

Toe-rag = salt cod
To Richard and Gilly Webb by way of thanks.

westcountry

Westcountry paint tins

All the colours in my tin
Go to paint the boat you're in
A bit of red bit of blue
White to let the rust show through
Orange as the sun it falls
Yellow for your overalls
I left the green till last you see
For green's the colour of the sea
The mighty sea may pick and choose
The colour that I need to use
Please little boat come safely back
And may I never use the colour black...

The sea, and indeed the river, has taken many people that I have known.

At the memorial service for Charles Causley

They gather here today
The people of the black and gold
One and all so soft spoken
To lend their love to a man
Who never wrote a love poem
Save to his mother
Save to twenty thousand children
Save to a sea of never forgotten souls
And to the places he loved
Which like his life ran
To seaward from the river ford
From where he watched them in silence
Those who walked across his life
Taught them letters and wrote of them
Touching so many
That in the cold church anointed by the
Biting Cornish rain which blew in
From the great winter grey Atlantic
Held at bay by Cornish granite
And coloured glass saints
We stood and sang
Strangers drawn in, yet at home
Made welcome to the church named for a woman
Who had washed the feet of Jesus
To pray and take tea,

In an assembly of those
More at home in great poet's parlour
Where they felt such a comfort
Called him Charles
As they read his soft saved chosen words
In their soft western voices
Pronounced from beyond the page
Brought to life the words
And smiled to themselves
When they recognised and remembered
Until they were done
And we filed outside
Past the black and white bookshop
In which his words will live
As long as Cornwall
To take tea and scones
In a clean church hall from church hall cups
That chinked as our spoons stirred in
Our first warm words to strangers
Spoken in hushed reverence
In our overcoats and oilskins
A western Sunday tea
On a wet Cornish Monday.

I share the love of Charles Causley's poetry with my daughter Robyn.
We just had to be at his memorial service.

China clay

Hatches up
Before she's alongside
It's a busy day and the jobs on the tide
There may be just enough time to touch up one side
Excepting it's not too wet or windy
Low water at lunch time it's a perfect day
As the tide returns again she'll be turned round and under way
The cranes are started and the jibs swing out
At the start of another day
It's cold and dry as the tide goes down
As the artic's come lumbering slowly down the hill into town
Lining the quay one by one
Those huge monsters in the still rising sun
With their huge stainless steel cups of china clay
Sixteen-wheeled oxen anxious to be emptied
And again on their way
There's no room for slackers along the quay
When they're loading the white gold of the Westcountry
Grey dust and grime all over the cabs
Tipping their loads under the grabs
Purring diesel engines as they wait their turn
For time is short and money to earn
By the hour
Keep it dry for they won't pay for water
The captains tetchy, the first mate his daughter
They'll keep them coming until the work is done

For dust dries quickly in the morning sun
Dust and noise is the order of the day
When a ship's in the port for the loading of china clay.
Is it for Russia is it for Spain?
They know her of old she'll be back again
Then the agents aboard the paperwork's done
And her lines are cast off
Before the heat's out of the sun
On comes the old pilot to take her to sea
They'll be kind to him, drop him off in under the lee
For the pilot boat's waiting, the ladder always slippery
As outward bound she passes with a final blast from her
horn
Passing another short sea trading ship inbound
She'll load on the morn
With her hatches up holds washed down
It's just another day in a china clay town...

To Ross, my son and everyone's sons and indeed daughters employed in the south-west's largest single export industry.

Fishermen

They are stealing from our fishermen
The will to go to sea
The blue and yellow pennants fly
To stop them going where they should be
Those hard men who brought the catches home
Their boats are sold and burnt
In the towns and villages where they grew to life
The shops are closed and barred
For the loss of money they once earned
The grey ghosts come to flay them bare
To hound them off the seas
And execute and talk of stupid rules laid down
In a foreign ministries
Whilst the Spanish and the Frenchy sail
Wherever they may please
And bend the rules to pinch the catch
With consummate European ease
And if our fishermen would do the same
Our ministers would see them shackled unemployed
And force them down upon on their knees
While those Brussels men in Brussels suits
Make rules in offices warm and sound
Making doubly sure that anyone but Englishmen
Can cast their nets across our British grounds

"Who cares what they say"
This is the west of England
Where it's hard to earn a pound
What future has the fisherman?
He who risks his life each day
Just more forms to fill in
And never extra pay
Our western brother is the fisherman
The farmer of the sea
He has fished the seas around the west
Since before our counties even had a name
And would it be too much to ask
Those bloody bureaucrats
That his children might do the very same...

Every time I pass the harbour in Newlyn and see good strong boats being broken up before their time I get very angry.

Cornish hymn

I have a love
She is not there
I sit beside her everywhere
She has no heart to give to me
She sits as stone beside the sea
Her shawl is blue, blue azure
Upon the morn
Her hair is red as twilight grows
Her hair is golden with the dawn
Her children sing
Of she they love
For she is Cornwall

St Piran's day.

How quickly the plough rusts

The now dull shears
That once uplifted sod
Acre after acre, day after day
Lay rusting in the farmyard
Where the cattle are gone
The stone walls are dry
There is nothing
Only the sound of the wind
As it blows, scratching dead brambles
A timeless plectrum strumming
Across the corrugated rooftops
In wintertime
What is there left to say save
"How quickly the plough rusts"

Written during the Foot and Mouth epidemic.

I could be over at Tesco's

I could be over at Tesco's
Doing the weekly shop
I could be over the Channel
Doing a Channel hop
It's no use you feeling sad
It's the route we have to choose
And it's ever so hard to stay really sad
When you're stocking up with booze
That's how I would like you to think of me
"Gone on a weekend cruise"
Yes gone where there is no housework
Nor any bills to pay
I am sorry I left in a hurry
I had to take it on the day
I saw it in the window
Scribbled up in thick black pen
It's time for you to leave it said
And join us now not when
So I'm just off to play tennis
With all the gang as before
That's how I need you to think of me
Just outside the door

Just outside the door
Where you will always be in my thoughts
I would love to stay
But I have to go
Or they'll fill up all the courts.

The sudden and untimely death of my friend Cllr Marjorie Tomlinson.

I pinched a pebble

I've pinched a pebble from the islands
I'll bring it back again each year
Then I'll pinch another pebble from the islands
It's just a loan
A way to keep the islands near
Sometimes in idle moments
I'll clasp it in my hand
Just to feel the warmth I crave
I'll need to pinch a pebble from the islands
Until they lay me in my grave
It feels so round and friendly
As I hold it close to me
I can feel through it the peace, the islands bring
And smell the clear cold sea
In this a tiny piece of Kernow's granite
That brings out the Celt in me
I need to pinch a pebble from the islands
Just to have it in my hand
I need to dream for just a moment of blue seas
And sugar white soft empty sand
Even when I am long gone
Perhaps there's no one left to know, that I did care
It will matter little

Because each and every pebble marks a someone
Who loved the islands
And who gave back their very last pebble
Then left their spirit lying there...

Thinking of the Isles of Scilly - to Melanie Woodcock, a woman with the gift of hospitality.

Last Saturday in October

All the townies in their greens
Standing by the cash machines
Row on row all wringing wet
Just as daft as daft can get
We have a little holiday home
Whoops there goes the mobile phone
Was it me or was it you
Mine's the four-track, what's to do
Let's all go and hunt down lunch
I know a place that at a crunch
Sits thirty
I am told it's where the locals go
All organic well you know
Gosh everyone looks just like me
Dressed in green beside the sea…

Anybody who lives in the Westcountry must be familiar with this scene.

London lunches

At London lunches the bigwigs decide
What gets ruined?
Or what floats out on the tide
What's in fashion!
And what is not
Who's to get nothing
And who's to get what
Our lives and futures
Comes in with the soup
As they in London decide how to recoup
What they will
Nothing changes it happens still
They eat their main course
They feed on us
By the time the pudding comes
The deals are done
And it's never them in London
Who pay the bill
It's us poor beggars in the provinces
And we are paying still.

Thinking of Appledore shipyard.

Miss Underhill

Miss Underhill didn't cite me in her will
Or set out to seek to thrill
She didn't take a man to bed
She gave the world so much more instead
And even now in my life she's a major feature
Miss Underhill was my English teacher
How she could lift the words right off the pages
Forget chemistry, history, and the Middle Ages
I was there
When the girl lay down with Laurie Lee
I drank the cider and the boy was me
What time had she to love a man
No woman with such a passion can
She was born to teach you see
To pluck the dry leaf from the tree
And give it life and make it shine
To lift the word beyond the page
Give it passion, excitement, rage
Then leave it safe inside your soul
Like a spent lover who again has control
Of their so enriched senses
Dear Miss Underhill we will never part
There a place for you right in my heart
Every time I read a poem late at night
It's your voice I hear when words excite

I wonder if you're still alive
I am fifty-three so you'll be eighty-five
I wonder then if it's too late
To ever to hear again you read with me
A piece from D.H.Lawrence, Christopher Marlow
Or Laurie Lee …

To Miss Underhill my English teacher and the reason why all good teachers look spent on Friday evenings.

Ode to Joyce Gundry's fruit cake

'Twas black as a Saint's cape
Yet tender as the light
As it rose like the sunlight which filled the bay
Over Porthleven on St Piran's day
Strong men would leave weak men
Lost in their wake
As they pulled home to the prize of
Mrs Joyce Gundry's fruit cake
The Lord in his heaven said
That looks rather nice
Do you think Mrs Gundry would save me a slice?
So the Almighty commanded
St Piran to stay
In the place where the waters run out to the bay
A cake I am promised from Mrs Gundry
Saying good Saint would you collect for it me
And in return this promise to Cornwall I make
A beautiful flag
In the shape of her cake
Just cut it in quarters
For all to see
One for the land

One for the sea
And one for all Cornishmen wherever they be
Last a piece for artists, miners and the poor fishermen
And save a piece for a poor poet whenever you can...

*In honour of my great friend Joyce Gundry who makes the best heavy fruit cake
in Cornwall.*

Ross Trebeer

Ross Trebeer
Stands on the Lizard headland cold and clear
And drinks in the Cornish morning
He does what he can with his old white van
Just to make a living
Bare-knuckle fighting in among the barn straw
And poetry for the main
Stone-walling in the summer light
Basket logs to the pubs
And trips to Brittany for cheap tobacco
Upon the Plymouth ferry
You see he's a Celt
And gets a belt from all things Cornish
He wheels and deals
Bends but never steals
Ross the man whose van proclaims on the side
Under the four black squares
That make up a white cross
Ross Trebeer bare-knuckle fighter and poet
Only in Cornwall would you see such a van
Only Cornwall as he sings like a bird
Would you meet such a man

To the Cornish where a poet could be a prince.

Mayday virgin

I am not from the land of light
And I will not dance
When the May flowers
Hold there heads tall
I will not dance
Nor will I follow that line
Or make passage
On that day when the flower
Is perfect
For although I love
The May flowers
The lily grows in another land
A land which is not mine by birth…

To my Cornish friends who invite me each year to Flora day. I choose not to go because I am not a Cornishman (I would love to come really!).

Sixteen-wheelers

I am the sixteen-wheeler
A man-made metal dynasty
I live to serve you my master
And feed your industry
I stand as high as heaven
And I sound like
The very devil's breath
As I deliver the cargo
To anywhere cargoes have to go
You may love me hate me curse me
But secretly you know
That's it's me who feeds the country
Takes what, where it has to go
Coal to warm your siblings
Fuel for you to waste
Be careful or I'll kill you,
If you overtake in haste
I line up on the dockside
At the container terminals I'm seen
Or dragging stone from quarries
To build that pretty house you're in
You will love me or hate me
As my turbo-diesel roars
'Cos I'm the super servant

The hydraulic dinosaur
I haul around the country
Twenty-four hours in the day
Everything from tarmac
To sand and dusty china clay
Don't blaspheme or cuss me
It's just a waste of time
'Cos I'm the sixteen-wheeler
Which you follow mile on mile
You may curse or abuse me each and every single day
And you can love me or hate me, I'll never go away
For I'm the girdered giant
Born of the blue electric arc
Who hisses smokes and frightens
Like a monster in the dark
You need me like you need a lover
To satisfy your greed
For I'm the dragon of commerce
The dirty filthy steed
You can neither beat me, or appease me
Nor will I ever go away
'Cos I do all your dirty work
And I am here to stay.

Dedicated to my good friend Mr Brian Chynoweth — a kindness returned.

Speed cameras

I'm the tin-box taxman
The camera up on high
A flasher for the government
As you go whizzing by
I'm the electric henchman
The silent iron triffid
Who sits atop my tower
I make the government millions
Hour on the hour
All I have to do is wait
Until you go hurrying by
Then I grab your hard-earned cash
I'm the government's little spy
I bleed the unsuspecting motorist
As though road tax ain't enough
It's easy money for the government
To waste on other stuff
I'm the secret penny-pincher
Who spreads his white-lined net
Some say it's "in the interest of safety"
Some say "it's for as much as I can get"
My brother was a dishwasher
My sister a TV
Mother was a capacitor
Who gave that little flash of light to me
The one that makes you miss a heartbeat

Wonder, I hope that was not me
I never sleep or call in sick
And I always earn my pay
I 'm less costly then a traffic cop
With no pension dues to pay
And I don't need any lunch breaks
Or expensive cars to drive around
I just sit here waiting patiently
With my one foot planted firmly in the ground
I'll snap you if you slip up
Just you wait and see
For I am the modern highway robber
No one gets past me

My friend Clare asked me to write a poem about speed cameras.

Westcountry woman

She spends her time as best she can
She runs her home for she has no man
She walks alone the cliffs, stares out to sea
She prays that he be safe wherever he be

Where is her husband, her lover, her man
Perhaps he's a soldier in a foreign land
Serving in jungles lush or hot desert sand
Or is he gone away over the endless sea
As so many have done from the Westcountry

It was like this since time recorded began
The western woman without her man
It's not her who sings "cheer up my lads"
And of the honours they won
With the bow the arrow the cannon, now the missile and gun

Who remembers them as they sit alone
Those Westcountry women who wait home
Waiting for news by the telephone
Hoping her husband is safe away out to sea
Seeing them fighting upon her TV

For the Westcountry woman it was ever so
The long days come, those same days go
For she stands in the shadow
Of all woman who wait
Watching the calendar marking the date
Until he returns

It was she who stood by the harbour side
Shone her lantern out into the dark sea so wide
She who huddled against the wind and raging sea
She who waved off the soldier dressed in khaki
She who watched as the lifeboat brought in the dead
Stood in dignified silence her heart full of dread.

For those Westcountry women
Who love Westcountry men
There is always the fear she'll not see him again
Bravely she holds back the tears, does not weep
That is until she's alone and the children asleep

Feel for her in her sorrow
She who pays for her love with her tears
Lives with the realisation of her very worst fears
Remember as you see that young woman in black
She's yet another Westcountry woman
Whose man's not coming back…

I admired the grit of Samantha Roberts, the Iraq war widow, and realised that she was joining so many women who have tragically seen their husbands go forth into danger, some sadly who were never to return.

Western moon

I stood on a beach with a western woman
Her soft grey eyes set on my own
And we talked as the seas lapped back and forth
In a land no longer now our home
We talked of a way of life all but gone
And our county's sad demise
And we watched as the sun turned red
As it went down
And raised up the star-filled skies
And we heard the call of the wise old owl
From the woods above the so still bay
And we talked fondly of the memories of our children
Now they had gone away
As we listened to the oyster catcher's final hurried call
Put an end to that western day
As silently we looked at what God had given us
What cash would take away
And we wondered what future
Our children would have for themselves
In the place they could not stay

We saw two silhouetted lovers holding hands
Walking lost in dreams toward the dunes
And we wished them the life we had
Under the western moon
We wished them a home

90

And a place to live
To raise up a family
In the lands where the red sun
Skims the ancient spirit-filled rocks
Then lights up the golden sea
And we cursed the banker and the city pound
That cuts us out like a knife
And we thought on the chains of hopelessness
Our children would drag
From now until the end of their life

And we wondered where they would love tonight
That couple mid the blue dark dunes
As they lay in each others arms, loved and dreamt
Without any hope of a future
Under the western moon.

A thought for Midsummer's Day.

The Devon flag

Across the soft breeze in gentle rhythm
Like the summer seas upon its shore
The warm janners' green flag flies
To mark this morning's coming day
St Petroc's long lost Celtic cross is found
The cruciform shape sea spume white
A calm white of saintly patients
The white of clay
Our flag which on stormy days cracks and shimmers
Up in the in the salt-caked crosstrees
Of a perhaps a thousand small ships
Marking those who have Devon in their hearts
May it watch over and guide our fishermen and seamen
Until they are safe again
Let it fly high on the church towers as the clock strikes
To bring the farmers
To the green fields which feed a nation
Dumnionia's flag
Its cross is laced with black
As is the moorland granite
The timeless headstone
Where they have carved our names in the past
And where we will remember those who have served our nation
Yet even as the flag was born...

Written for the people of the county of Devon.

INDEX

ACKNOWLEDGEMENTS

My thanks go out to the following.

I am drawn to strong women. Many who have played a huge part in my life. My late wife Lyzie could be outrageous and very funny yet if she said *no* and looked at you with those blue eyes fixed on your own it was a *no* which was cast in granite!

If it were not for Caroline Drew taking the time to mark and correct my first rambling poetical drafts and encourage me to continue writing my poems I would never have achieved the dream of my poems in print. Despite over twenty years away from teaching she is still a teacher at heart.

Sarah Flint, again a teacher and long term friend, for lending her time to me whilst walking me slowly away from my loss.

Clare Thorp, also a good friend, who shares my confidence and my love of the sea and who features in some of the poems. She has the best sea-sense of anyone I know.

Jo Unwin (Lyzie's nearest sister by age - she had three), a fellow dreamer and photographer, for just being Jo. Photography, with Jo and Lyzie's guidance, taught me to look at what I see.

Mrs Lin Lloyd (aunty) and Maggie Trubshaw for the hours of laughter, mainly spent in Cornwall following the pilot gigs, both when Lyzie was alive and after her death. Thanks for the suppers.

My thanks also to the entire Dart ladies B pilot gig crew (Lyzie's crew) who trained on roll-ups and red wine and won every race everywhere they competed on the Cornish circuit that season in which Lyzie left us. I was their groupie.

Thanks also to my daughter Robyn for being the beneficiary of many of my hare-brained schemes. It can't be easy having a prodigal father. I know you must miss your mum so much. You have your mother's warm smile.

And to Ross my ever patient son who sorted out again and again my documentation when it had gone into hiding inside my ageing computer. It's a lucky man who can say he admires his son and daughter and all they have achieved. I love you both.

I thank the many doctors and nurses who tended me and kept me alive when I should have died recently. Thanks, also, to all my friends who supported me at that time, including my boyhood friend Tony Mulliken. The world needed a self-opinionated, ex-ferryman with a gammy leg and a balding head so very much.

My thanks also go out to Richard and Gilly Webb both busy people who took time to look at my poems and gifted me the chance to see them in print and share them with others. They are both passionate about the Westcountry and true river lovers'. More than this they gave me back a shape and purpose to my life.

The photograph of my old dog Ceilidh and me on the back cover is by Ski Harrison taken on what turned out to be a great day out on the river.

Lastly my sincere thanks to Alice Oswald, poet and wordsmith. We were fated by chance and the river Dart to meet (I am her ferryman). It was Alice who first told me that I was a poet. Nothing anyone has ever said except perhaps that first whispered *I love you* from a then seventeen-year-old Lyzie and the birth of our children, has meant more to me.

Each one of you is mentioned in my poems or have poems written with you in mind. You will know who you are. I am privileged to call all of you my friends.

I dedicate the poems in this book to my lovely Lyzie and to anyone who has beautiful ideas trapped inside their head - yet cannot through their lack of word-skills or fluency say exactly what they mean or put them down on paper. It can be an awful burden to carry.

Kevin Pyne

I took the photos illustrated on the front cover and the endpapers and they show the following:
Front cover: My daughter Robyn rowing our white dinghy 'Poppy' on the river Dart on a memorable summer's day (see my poem 'Rowing the white boat' on page 34).
Inside front cover: My late wife Lyzie on her 43rd birthday - one of my favourite pictures of her.
Inside back cover: My son Ross (in orange shirt) with his gig-rowing friends on the accompanying blue fishing boat, at the County Gig Championships, Newquay.